free space

a perspective on the small group in women's liberation

pamela allen

Printed in U.S.A.
Second Edition, revised

Times Change Press
62 W. 14 St., NY NY 10011

SBN 87810-006-7

Photographs by Pamela Allen
Photograph of Pam by
        Robert & Pamela Allen

Cover photograph by Irene Peslikis

CONTENTS

INTRODUCTION

After three years of being in the women's movement I understand that one of the basic needs which drove me to join women's liberation was a need to do meaningful work—work that encouraged self growth and at the same time was relevant to other people's needs. I have long believed in the basic value of the small group for women's liberation but all my life I have felt tremendously inadequate to the task of writing and thus it has taken me two years of psychological preparation and six months of physical work to write my ideas on the small group. Many women have been asking what happens in a small group and why some people feel that it is an important structure for women's liberation. This handbook—its pictures and its words—is my attempt to communicate what a small group experience has meant to me and why. I have written it particularly for women beginning the small group experience and for women who are already in small groups but have not formulated a satisfying definition for themselves. Hopefully you will find the ideas stimulating, some of the concepts relevant to your needs. I hope that this will be the beginning of a dialogue between us.

I joined my group—Sudsofloppen—at its second meeting in September 1968. I was new to San Francisco, having moved from New York City where I had been active in women's liberation. I brought to the group a political commitment to building a mass women's movement. The group experience has helped me to synthesize and deepen my emotional and intellectual understanding of the predicament of being female in this society and the concerns with which we must deal in building a women's movement.

We have defined our group as a place in which to think: to think about our lives, our society and our potential for being creative individuals and for building a women's movement. We call this Free Space. We have had successes and failures in utilizing this space. Usually our problems stem from our failures to be completely honest with ourselves and each other—failing to accept the responsibility to question and disagree with another's ideas and perspective and saying what we think is an alternative. Our failures to be truthful have always had a negative effect on the functioning of our group. Thus individual integrity—intellectual and emotional honesty—is our goal. It has been and is a difficult struggle.

Precisely because the group does become so meaningful to our lives as we start to separate ourselves from dependence on male values and institutions, it is a temptation to transfer our identities onto the group, to let our thinking be determined by group consensus rather than doing it ourselves. Although we are not sure that full autonomy is a possible goal, we do believe that our hope lies in developing as individuals who understand themselves, their own needs, the workings of our society and the needs of others. Thus we try to resist the temptation to submerge our individuality within the group and struggle instead to try to make contact with our own feelings and thoughts. Freedom is frightening and difficult to use. We are always struggling to take advantage of the Free Space we have created for ourselves.

We have developed four group processes to help us in our endeavors to become autonomous in our thinking and behavior. We call these processes opening up, sharing, analyzing and abstracting. They are our way of keeping in touch with our emotions, giving one another information regarding experiences we have had, trying to understand the meaning of those events, and finally fitting that understanding into an overview of our potential as human beings and the reality of our society, i.e. of developing an ideology.

The group processes are described in length in the third chapter. It should be understood that they are not totally separate processes. Rather there is a great deal of overlap but the emphasis in opening up is on our feelings, in sharing on our experiences, in analyzing on our thinking and in abstracting on our evolving theory.

I have attempted to use the processes to describe my experiences and thinking as a member of Sudsofloppen. This introduction is my attempt to show you how I feel about my group experience. It has given me the courage and strength to write this handbook and it has constantly challenged me to be honest with myself regarding my own needs and the needs of others. The following chapters will tell what happened in our group, what my thinking is about Free Space, the group process, the group's relation to the individual woman and to the women's movement, and finally my approach to developing a comprehensive ideology from which to operate. Lastly, I have included in an appendix a paper written by the group as a whole describing who we were and where we wanted to go at the end of our first six months together.

This is the second edition of Free Space, the first being published in May, 1970. I have made considerable changes in the content of the first two chapters. This edition includes fewer details regarding our group and movement activity and stresses the general trends instead. This is because the details of our activities have changed as we have developed our movement and they do not contribute significantly to the main points I am trying to cover in this handbook.

The handbook is based on the following premises. First I believe that women are oppressed by society and by individual men, that they are beginning to rise against that oppression and have the potential of forming a social movement of historic proportions. However, for this to be successful we must develop an ideology and learn to think autonomously. Secondly I believe that there are basic differences in perception between men and women because women do not have the social and economic advantages that men do. Although we may live intimately together, men and women relate in terms of men having the ultimate power. There is a women's point of view, a women's reality. It is the reality of an oppressed people and it is not acknowledged by our society because this would attest to the fact that women's and men's equality is a myth.

I have chosen to write about one structure that has developed in the women's movement, the small group, because I think that the small group is especially suited to freeing women to affirm their view of reality and to learn to think independently of male supremacist values. It is a space where women can come to understand not only the ways this society works to keep women oppressed but also ways to overcome that oppression psychologically and socially. It is Free Space.

Pamela Allen

Peggy

SUDSOFLOPPEN

We are the oldest group in our city; thus when we started we were very alone in working out a definition for ourselves. The definition we have evolved of the small group as Free Space has been the result of all of us changing our views. It is a synthesis of what seemed originally to be contradictory approaches to working towards liberation. Free Space is the testament to our collective thinking and to our growth as individuals through experiencing the group process. Our struggle to reach this definition has not been easy. It was a difficult struggle, especially at the beginning.

When our group began about half the women were friends but all of us knew at least one other person in the group since word of the group's formation was communicated only through personal contact. Within a few meetings we settled into a fairly regular membership of about a dozen women. For five months we talked together. In those early meetings we talked a great deal about how we perceived the role of women in our society, our attitudes towards ourselves and other women, our very real problems with men in our private lives and on our jobs and, of course, what we hoped the group could be for us. Many women wanted the group to become a large family where needs could be met that were not being met in their private lives (homes—communes) and jobs. This meant that the group was being asked to offer women meaning for their lives, companionship and trust, and guidance to function creatively. But many things stood in our way, especially our own self-hatred and resentment toward others, our impatience and naivete about the difficulties involved in making changes and our

11

disagreements about the way to approach our liberation.

During those first months together we discovered how hard it is to change old ways of behaving, even when they are detrimental to us and to other women. And we found that our own fears of inadequacy made us intolerant of others' weaknesses or jealous of others' strengths. We came to learn the hard way that one of the key characteristics of an oppressed people is self hatred, and that our tendency to take out our frustrations on one another was a sign of our oppression. In time we came to see that there is a difference between resentment and anger. Resentment comes from feeling inferior, especially to men. As we became more sure of ourselves and the accuracy of our perceptions, we became less resentful. We still felt (and feel) anger towards the oppressive actions of individual men and social institutions but we were less resentful, for they no longer had power over us. Resentment towards ourselves and other women was more difficult to overcome. Until we understood what resentment was we could not even face these feelings within ourselves. We now understand that striking out at other women for being weak (or strong) comes from our own fears of weakness, but that objective criticism is constructive and necessary if we are to grow in strength.

Our lack of understanding of the complexities of our condition and the difficulties in trying to change one's life, was exemplified in our assumption, stated many times in the group, that if we all felt the same alienation, the same burden of being female, then the simple act of getting together would alleviate our pain. It did not. Recognizing the pain in another as one's own does not free one of pain. To know that you are not alone is a freeing experience because it can give you hope. But this knowledge in no way changes objective reality. Society still functions the same way and on the whole, so do we.

The greatest cause of tension in our group was the disagreement regarding how liberation could be accomplished—personally or politically. Some said that liberation would come through changing ourselves; thus we should talk about our private lives and our feelings towards ourselves and each other. Others felt that liberation would come by first changing our society; thus we should talk about building a political women's movement. The women who felt that our first and most important task was to change ourselves by growing in self awareness and developing more honest personal relationships, felt that politics were irrelevant if not detrimental to human liberation. They based this on their past experiences in New Left politics (and, of course, from viewing Establishment politics) where they saw people being inhuman to one another in the name of progress and humanity. These women saw this as being in absolute contradiction to the movement's professed goal of learning to be loving and responsive people. For these women politics became equated with inhumanity. But others (and I was one of these) believed that no real changes could be made in our lives unless these changes were societal. We felt that our strength would be in our numbers and that a few women trying to change their personal lives would be too vulnerable. We wanted to build an effective political movement that could both confront the injustices of our society and also protect the right of individual women to change their life styles.

Slowly we came to see that both approaches were necessary, interdependent, and doomed to failure if attempted alone. This became clear as we began to see the social causes of our personal problems and, in the case of those of us who had begun to act politically, the personal causes of our political problems. We found that the group was not healthy when isolated from other women's groups and that we as individuals could not escape the male supremacy of our society. In addition those of us who had begun to act in our developing women's movement in San Francisco, found that our feelings towards ourselves and other women, our level of emotional understanding and maturity, very much affected

13

our political abilities. Thus we came to see the necessity of our group not only being a part of a women's movement but a place where we would constantly develop our intellectual and emotional understanding of our society and of ourselves. The group became the place where our personal lives and our political lives could meet. For women like myself this meant being willing to share more of our personal selves in the group; for others it meant being willing to relate impersonally in the realm of ideas. For all of us it took faith to move into areas we feared.

What was it that we feared; that originally made each side so sure that the other had been wrong? It seems to me now that we all lacked trust in ourselves and we feared that if we let go of that aspect of women's liberation that already meant so much to us (whether it be personal relationships or political understanding) that we would lose what we had. In those early days we did not have the wisdom to see that growth stagnates if isolated. Nor did we have the faith to believe that we would enhance our growth in the areas most dear to us not by denying other facets of ourselves, but rather by developing them also.

We came to accept that we are individuals with emotional needs and fears (no matter how hard we tried to hide them behind intellectual endeavors), and that we live in a society which has power over the individual (no matter how hard we tried to hide from that reality in personal relationships). It seems so clear to us now that relationships do not grow in a vacuum but through experiencing the whole of life together, and that a human politics will not grow from people who fear honest human relationships but through ones who are willing to share of their total selves. We also realized, however, that it would take years to work out the answers to our many needs and that our growth, if it was to be balanced and sustaining, would have to be slow. There could be no quick, simplistic answers if we were serious about making real changes in our lives and in our society.

We found that not all the women in our group were able to make the decision to have the group be the place where all facets of ourselves could meet, accepting that our progress would be slow but more balanced. Those of us who have stayed have found our faith rewarded. We have indeed grown, more than we did in those early months, both in our love for one another and in our understanding of our society. We think the love his grown because we stopped looking self consciously for it and began to struggle together instead. And our beginning to relate to our society through the women's movement has given a central unity to our lives. We are no longer drifting, relating passively to life; rather we are attempting through an intense relationship to society to affect history, to act instead.

Perhaps the only truth I can say to others is that we have had to learn that progress is slow, our mistakes many. To heal and restore ourselves to wholeness and to help change this society—these are goals which may well take a lifetime before they are achieved. We in Sudsofloppen have committed ourselves to offering each other a space each week to evaluate our progress and to grow in understanding. Our comradeship is growing through struggling together and our hope is sustained through our collective vision.

Linda

FREE SPACE

We have come to see that being human means growing both in the realm of personal relationships and in the realm of ideas and skills. If this growth is attempted alone or in superficial situations, it is usually only growth in the areas where we are already the strongest. In addition if we relate only to our family members or friends, we are not challenged to develop new facets of ourselves either. It is when we come into a long term relationship with people with whom we don't associate regularly that the old roles we play can be set aside for a space in which we can develop ourselves more fully as whole human beings. Free Space is the meeting ground of our many lives; it is a collective meeting ground because in honest relationship with others, we expand our perspectives and can reach new levels of consciousness.

The group experience as Free Space is based on trust and honesty; to develop trust is the first prerequisite to utilizing Free Space. Trust is what gives us the strength to be honest; trust in oneself and in one's sisters in the group. We have found, however, that trust is not easy to develop in the group. There are many roadblocks in our way, probably the most important being our fear of taking ourselves and each other seriously. In addition, not liking one woman's personality, fearing that another may be emotionally immature and will prove a drain on the group, finding someone's ideas naive or stupid or feeling that someone is pushing you—all these reactions can inhibit the building of trust.

Building trust is a slow process that grows through seeing each other live up to the commitments we make. If a group values commitment as a sign of responsibility to the group, usually those women who cannot give to others and only want the group to meet their own needs will withdraw from membership, leaving the group free to develop the trust that each member will try to live up to the group commitments. Originally, in the early months of our group, we talked of commitment to the group in very grandiose terms—we would meet all of the needs each of us had that were not being met elsewhere. But we learned that there are some commitments that it was impossible for us to meet, such as offering a woman a meaningful private life, and that there were other commitments which were very much within our abilities that we would overlook, such as attending meetings on time. I remember that my first trust in the group developed through seeing the women bring the food for the dinners we had together before our meetings. In those early days I was distrustful of our talk about love and unwilling to trust my whole self with a group of strangers, but I was willing to risk a meal. And the fact that I never went hungry—week after week—made me begin to trust that we could begin to feed each other's need for a place to be taken seriously and for a space to learn about ourselves and grow in understanding and strength.

We no longer eat together before meetings because it began to take too much time from our meetings, but we have continued to be aware that trust is sustained and grows through seeing each other act responsibly towards the group. Our first commitment to one another is to attend meetings regularly. We come to meetings on time and call if we will be late. We try to inform the group ahead of time if we will miss a meeting. We utilize our meeting time of three hours to the best of our abilities and end on time. We have found that concentrating our meeting time on what is important to us has made the meetings more meaningful and less draining than rambling chatter. We try to contribute to the development of the group's ideas both by doing individual thinking ahead of time and by taking other people's ideas seriously. And always, we try to be aware of the individual needs of our members, both by giving a space for talk and perspective and by helping concretely when we can. In this last area individuals in the group help to care for the children of the two mothers in the group—once we did this for four days so that the mother could get a vacation. Also the group has given me some financial aid so that I could put full time effort into this handbook.

Some of the examples of commitments stated above may seem trivial; they are not. It does make a difference to know that we are a group, that each week we will meet together. No other trust can develop if we cannot even trust that our group is a reality. It is not probable that women will trust their most deep feelings or ideas to women of whose presence at the next meeting they are not even sure. The stability of a group's membership is essential and continuity is also important. We feel that women should start at the beginning with a group if possible so that they do not miss any of the essential early group experiences. We closed our group to new people after a few months because we felt that we needed this continuity. After making this decision however, we did bring another woman into the group and later two sisters who came to San Francisco from groups in the East. We did not attempt to get to know each other however, assuming somehow that they would just become integrated into our group. All three chose to leave us during the time we reached our definition of our group as Free Space. They all went into other groups that more nearly fit their needs and we became even more convinced of the difficulty of integrating new members into an already functioning group. Our thinking now is that for a new person to successfully come into an already established group she needs to have been in a group previously which has had a similar history and she needs to know and agree with the definition that the group has of itself. Lastly the group must spend time getting to know the new member emotionally and intellectually. This must take precedence over all other group activity if the new sister is to be integraged. We used this method to bring in a new member in the fall of 1969 and feel that is has indeed worked; that Kathy is now an equal member of Sudsofloppen.

Meeting together weekly is no guarantee that honesty and growth will occur nor that Free Space will develop. I think that faith is as important an ingrediant as commitment. We must believe in ourselves as individuals and as a group if we are to trust one another enough to be honest. Since we do not always live up to our aspirations, this means we must have faith that each is trying and that progress will occur. Our expectations must be realistic, we must understand the pressures and obligations under which our members are living. If we expect too much of one another we will be disappointed but at the same time, we must constantly challenge each other to develop our untapped potential if we are to grow.

Part of the reason we in Sudsofloppen are able to have faith in the group is that we ask no more of each other than to fulfill our group commitment of making a Free Space. We do not ask group members to fulfill our needs for a satisfying private life because we value the chance for space away from the people to whom we have made personal commitments. Some of our members used to live together but we found that this detracted both from the group experience and from their personal relationships. The group is based on the faith that we will affirm each other regardless of our weaknesses and failures in our daily struggles, and will work towards an understanding of our predicament of being female in this society. Because this is our commitment to one another we are emotionally free to forgive each other's failures in other areas.

Free Space is free because we do relate apart from our daily. lives. This does not mean that some of us do not have friendships together outside the group meetings; we do. But our first commitment to each other is our group commitment and we have allowed our friendships to grow only as we have felt strong enough to meet these new obligations to one another.

In our group we are a gathering of equals who have left behind our daily cares for a short while and participate in the collective building of ideas together. Having established trust through our commitment to the group, we can look upon life from a vantage point that gives us, first, a perspective and, as we grow together, a framework for our thinking. We use thought processes and assumptions developed by the group as a whole, but each of us, with our unique (special) viewpoint on life, contributes to that thought process.

Susan

THE SMALL GROUP PROCESS

The group processes described in this chapter were discussed and identified by Sudsofloppen after we had been meeting for over a year. This was one of the first times that we turned our growing ability to analyze onto ourselves and our own activity. The experience of working out these concepts collectively was very exciting for us all. The processes may seem a little arbitrary and too structured for some of you but we are a group which believes that there is always a structure, the issue is to consciously choose one that will encourage our growth rather than just hope that it will happen. We think this way because our early activity was consciously unstructured—we thought—and we found that letting things just happen meant that the strongest personalities controlled the meetings and that it was very easy to avoid areas of discussion that were difficult. The group processes as described here are impersonal and they ensure that those of us who find it hard to open up about our feelings will be challenged to do so. The same is true for women who fear analysis and would rather stay only on the subjective level. The total process is not easy but we feel that *each* process is necessary to understanding the human experience. We believe that theory and analysis which are not rooted in concrete experience (practice) are useless, but we also maintain that for the concrete, everyday experiences to be understood, they must be subjected to the processes of analysis and abstraction.

OPENING UP

This is a very individual need: the need for a woman to open up and talk about her feelings about herself and her life. In the beginning of a group experience opening up is a reaching out to find human contact with other women. Later it becomes a way to communicate to others about one's subjective feelings—about the group, about the women's movement, about one's life.

Our society alienates us from our feelings. However, this is less true for women than for men. It is imperative for our understanding of ourselves and for our mental health that we maintain and deepen our contact with our feelings. Our first concern must not be with whether these feelings are good or bad but what they are. Feelings are a reality. To deny their existence does not get rid of them. Rather it is through admitting them that one can begin to deal with her feelings.

Opening up is an essential but difficult process for a group. In its early stages a group usually fosters a feeling of intimacy and trust which frees women to discuss their fears and problems. This is because most women have been isolated and alone and the group experience is the first time they have found others who like themselves are frustrated with their lot as women in this society. Every woman who has tried to articulate her loss of a sense of identity to her husband knows the despair of not being understood. Any woman who has tried to explain her driving need to have a life of her own and sees her words falling on the incomprehending ears of family and friends knows the horror of being alone, being seen by others as some kind of freak. Any woman who has admitted that she is unhappy and depressed but can't explain why, knows the pain of not being taken seriously. Isolated, always getting negative responses to her attempts to communicate her feelings about her condition, it is very easy to begin to question herself, to see her problems in personal terms.

The group offers women a place where the response will be positive. "Yes, we know." "Yes, we understand." It is not so much the words that are said in response that are important; rather it is the fact that someone listens and does not ridicule; someone listens and acknowledges the validity of another's view of her life. It is the beginning of sisterhood, the feeling of unity with others, of no longer being alone.

The early group experience of closeness—the honeymoon period as some call it—fosters opening up about one's feelings towards oneself and one's life. But as the group begins to function on a long term basis and the members participate in activities in a women's movement, it becomes harder to be honest about one's feelings for sometimes they are negative and may involve another woman. Yet such disclosures are necessary if trust and sisterhood are to become long term realities. Neither a group nor a movement can function if there is latent distrust and hostility or overt back biting going on. In addition an individual cannot be free to trust in herself and in others if she is suppressing feelings and allowing them to cloud her thinking and activity.

Opening up is a personal need to admit to and express one's emotions—her joys as well as her sorrows. In addition it is a group need in that no group can continue to function over a long period of time which does not deal with the feelings of its members. Unless women are given a *non-judgmental* space in which to express themselves, we will never have the strength or the perception to deal with the ambivalences which are a part of us all. It is essential that the group guarantee confidentiality; that we know that our feelings will not be told elsewhere or used against us. This is a group commitment without which there can be no trust.

SHARING

The opening up process is centered on the individual's expressive needs, and carried to an extreme it can become self indulgence. However, there is another experience that can take place in the group which is similar to the first yet different, for the emphasis is on teaching one another through sharing experiences. Not only do we respond with recognition to someone's account, but we add from our own histories as well, building a collage of similar experiences from all women present. The intention here is to arrive at an understanding of the social conditions of women by pooling descriptions of the forms oppression has taken in each individual's life. Revealing these particulars may be very painful, but the reason for dredging up these problems is not only for the therapeutic value of opening up hidden areas. Through experiencing the common discussion comes the understanding that many of the situations described are not personal at all, and are not based on individual inadequacies, but rather have a root in the social order. What we have found is that painful "personal" problems can be common to many of the women present. Thus attention can turn to finding the real causes of these problems rather than merely emphasizing one's own inadequacies.

Almost any topic can be used for the sharing process. All that is necessary is that women have experience in that area. Some of the topics we have used for discussion have been communal living, job experiences, movement experiences in civil rights, SDS and the peace movement, relationships with men focusing on examples of male chauvinism, relationships with women with emphasis on our adolescent experiences and how these affect our present feelings toward women, and our self images—how we perceive ourselves and how we think others perceive us. Agreeing on a topic, and preparing for the discussion for a week or so, seems to ensure the most productive sharing discussion.

The sharing occasions have shown us that the solutions to our problems will be found in joining with other women, because the basis of many of our problems is our status as women. It was not only sharing the stories of our childhood, school, marriage and job experiences which led us to this realization. It was as much the positive feelings, the warmth and comradeship of the small group which reinforced the conviction that it is with other women both now and in the future that solutions will be found. The old stereotypes that women can't work together and don't like one another are shown to be false in practice.

After sharing we *know* that women suffer at the hands of a male supremacist society and that this male supremacy intrudes into every sphere of our existence, controlling the ways in which we are allowed to make our living and the ways in which we find fulfillment in personal relationships. We know that our most secret, our most private problems are grounded in the way women are treated, in the way women are allowed to live. Isolation turns frustration into self doubt; but joining together gives women perspective that can lead to action. Through sharing they can see that they have been lied to, and begin to look critically at a society which so narrowly defines the roles they may play. But before they can take their destinies into their own hands, they must understand the objective condition of women and the many forms that oppression takes in the lives of women.

ANALYZING

A third stage now takes place in the group: the experience of analyzing the reasons for and the causes of the oppression of women. This analysis rises out of the questions which are posed by the basic raw data of the opening up and sharing periods. It is a new way of looking at women's condition: the development of concepts which attempt to define not only the why's and how's of our oppression but possible ways of fighting that oppression. Because the analysis takes place *after* the sharing of individual examples of oppression, it is based on a female understanding of the reality of women's condition.

This period is important because it is the beginning of going beyond our personal experiences. Having gained a perspective on our lives through the sharing process, we now begin to look at women's predicament with some objectivity. This new approach is difficult for many of us as our lives as women exist predominantly in the realm of subjectivity; we perform functions but seldom get on top of a situation to understand how something works and why. This is a new and difficult procedure to learn.

In analyzing the role the group has played in our lives, for example, we have come to understand the ways in which women are kept from feeling they are worthwhile. We have discussed the need to have a social identity and how women are prevented from aquiring one. Women's roles as wife and mother have been analyzed. We have come to see that women are relegated to a private sphere, dependent both psychologically and financially on their husbands. The group is a first step in transcending the isolation. Here sometimes for the first time in her life a woman is allowed an identity independent of a man's. She is allowed to function intellectually as a thinker rather than as a sex object, servant, wife or mother. In short, the group establishes the social worth of the women present, a necessity if women are to take themselves seriously.

We have had to face realistically the inability of many of us to think conceptually. This inability comes from being encouraged to stay in the private sphere and to relate to people on personal levels even when working. We are training ourselves to get out from under our subjective responses and look at our reality in new ways. Although this is not easy for us, we see the absolute necessity of analysis, for our oppression takes both obvious and subtle forms which vary depending on our class and educational status. The complexity of women's situations necessitates that we bring information outside of our individual experiences to bear on our analysis of women's oppression. This is the period when questions can be asked about how the entire society functions. This is the period when books and other documentation become crucial.

It is our contention, however, that this period of analysis belongs *after* the opening up and sharing experiences, for concepts we find must answer the questions which come from our problems as women. It is not in our interest to fit experiences into preconceived theory, especially one devised by men. This is not only because we must suspect all male thinking as being male supremacist, but also because we must teach ourselves to think independently. Our thinking must grow out of our questions if it is to be internalized and if we are to have the tools to look objectively at new experience and analyze that correctly. Thus a period of analysis will come after each new experience and will add new thinking to an ever growing ideology.

ABSTRACTING

A synthesis of the analyses is necessary before decisions can be made as to priorities in problems and approach. For this to happen a certain distance must exist between us and our concerns. When we remove ourselves from immediate necessity, we are able to take the concepts and analysis we have developed and discuss abstract theory. We are able to look at the totality of the nature of our condition, utilizing the concepts we have formulated from discussions of the many forms our oppression takes. Further we begin to build (and to some extent, experience) a vision of our human potential. This does not mean we become more like men.

Rather we come to understand what we could be if freed of social oppression. We see this abstracting experience as the purest form of Free Space.

We are only beginning to experience this Free Space, abstracting, now that we have a year of opening up, sharing, and analyzing behind us. We are beginning to see how different institutions fulfull or prevent the fulfillment of human needs, how they work together and how they must be changed. We are beginning to gain an overview of what type of women's movement will be necessary to change the institutions that oppress women. Specifically we have begun to have a clear understanding of what role the small group can and cannot play in this social revolution. It is clear to us that the small group is neither an action-oriented political group in and of itself nor is it an alternative family unit. Rather this is where ideology can develop. And out of this emerging ideology will come a program grounded in a solid understanding of women's condition which will have its roots, but not its totality, in our own experience. Intellectually this is the most exciting stage. It is a joy to learn to think, to begin to comprehend what is happening to us. Ideas are experiences in themselves, freeing, joyous experiences which give us the framework for formulating our actions.

It is important to stress that opening up, sharing, analyzing and abstracting are not limited to certain periods of time. One never completes any of the processes. Opening up is not limited to the past and one does not graduate through the various processes until one is only abstracting to the exclusion of all else. Analyzing and abstracting are only valid processes if they continue to be rooted in the present feelings and experiences of participants. The order may be fixed but the processes themselves are ongoing.

The total group process is not therapy because we try to find the social causes for our experiences and the possible programs for changing these. But the therapeutic experience of momentarily relieving the individual of all responsibility for her situation does occur and is necessary if women are to be free to act. This takes place in both the opening up and sharing phases of the group activity and gives us the courage to look objectively at our predicament, accepting what are realistically our responsibilities to change and understanding what must be confronted societally.

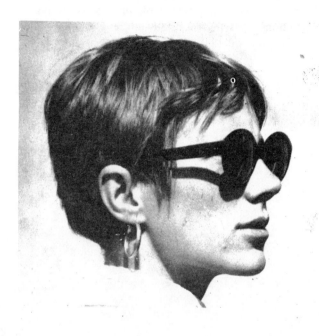

Pat

THE INDIVIDUAL AND THE SMALL GROUP

We have said earlier that for women's liberation to be achieved it is necessary to change ourselves and our society. Before we can know how to change either, however, we must understand our own needs. Women's needs are more complex than our society admits. First we have a need for a financially secure, satisfying and stable private life. Second we need outlets for creativity which have social relevance, i.e. which exist outside the world of our private life. And third we need a framework for perceiving our reality, an ideology based on the premise of our self worth as individuals who are women.

It is not the purpose of this handbook to discuss in detail the condition of women in our society but to suggest a vehicle for women to use to arrive at that understanding themselves. However, no understanding of the individual needs of women can be divorced from the social and economic reality of our society. It should be sufficient for our purposes to note that this society teaches that women are to find their meaning in life in marriage and child-rearing, justifying social and economic discrimination on this assertion. The median incomes of both black and white women are lower than those of both black and white men even though the median education of both groups of women is higher than their male counterparts. The majority of jobs open to women are in service and menial occupations; much of the work is repetitious, boring and hard. The pay is low and there is little chance for women to earn a decent living, much less find meaning in their work. Women work because they must, but they earned a median income 58% that of men in 1966, for example. The reasons for marriage then stem as much from economic pressures as from social pressures, the latter being very familiar to all women.

The needs of a private life are what are usually considered the primary needs; shelter, food, companionship, understanding and sex (which has to be in the spirit of stability and intimacy). Usually these find some fulfillment in a family structure (communal as well as nuclear) and they necessitate one or more of the family members earning money. I would also include the needs for friendship, fellowship, and play which find expression outside intimate living arrangements as well. Living arrangements are satisfactory in terms of how many of the above needs are being met. Although these needs can never be fully satisfied since the oppression of women very much pervades the private realm where women are unpaid domestic and sexual servants, the establishment of some type of satisfactory living arrangement is a basic individual need. Each woman must find ways to have these needs met. The group defined as Free Space would not meet these needs, nor would the group tell an individual woman what choices she can or cannot make. However, the group can help her gain perspective on her life and the possible solutions to her problems.

A second form of individual experience necessary if we are to be full people is the experience of actualizing ourselves in work which is not only meaningful to ourselves but has meaning to others as well. This process in a capitalist society is denied to all but the privileged few (the majority white males). As women it is denied us almost totally. Creative work can take many forms but involves achievement, self discipline, autonomy and the ability to function in a social context. It is important not only because it contributes to the good of others but also because in taking place in a larger world context, it allows us to transcend our own subjective lives and function on the level of skills and ideas. It is this lack of opportunity to do socially relevant work which makes women's home lives doubly oppressive, for not only are we the servants of husband and children but we have no social outlets for our creativity. (Childrearing was once work that was socially valued but even then it was not considered women's only work. Today large families are no longer economic necessities and are disfunctional both in terms of mobility and in limiting the population growth. Thus the one meaningful aspect of women's role in the home is losing its meaning.)

Again the group is not the place for this human need to be productive to be fulfilled. Contributing to the group process does not replace this need to contribute to the world at large. That is one reason we need a women's movement. With very few exceptions individual women will not be able to find the opportunity to contribute in productive ways to society or be able to affect concrete changes and do work which has relevance to other women within society's institutions. These kind of jobs do not exist for women in a male supremacist society and although women may have to work to earn a living (to fulfill their private life needs) they will have to look elsewhere for meaningful work. Giving a few women token jobs will not change this. For us meaningful work must take the form of changing society itself.

The third need that women share with all humans is the need for a framework from which to operate. We as individuals need a way to understand our experiences and the world around us. This includes understanding the interrelations between economic reality and human nature. The society in which we live has an ideology which it teaches its young. It is a justification for economic control being in the hands of a few. It is a white male supremacist ideology because it justifies the exploitation of women and nonwhites for the benefit of white males.

We need an ideology that affirms the right of all people to share equally in the obligations and benefits of our society. The small group is a structure which can offer us a reference point from which to operate. Such an ideology will be directly related to the reality of being human as women experience it. I am speaking here not only of perspective but indeed a whole framework for viewing the world, our society and our place in it. It is imperative that women evolve an ideology if they are ever to become autonomous and capable of acting independently. This will not come easily but the small group process is well suited towards helping this to happen.

It is important that I stress that I do not mean the group will develop this ideology for its members. If we are to become autonomous thinkers, each individual must work out her own framework for herself. The group offers a space and a structure for individuals to use but the basic growth is as individuals. The goal of the group should not be to force each member into one mold. Nor should the group allow its members to forego the struggle of learning to think by allowing them to unquestioningly adopt someone else's ideas. Rather the group experience is stimulus to self growth. Differences should be explored, alternative perspectives encouraged, for our goal is autonomous women, not women dependent on a group for ideology. This means that each individual must do her own work and thinking. Although there may seem to be many differences within a group, I think that a lot of these will prove to be individual perspectives of the same reality. In addition, the group does not exist in isolation from society and our understanding will grow closer as we work together to confront the inequalities of our society. We are all women struggling together and we confront the same society with its contradictions. Sharing many individual perspectives will give us all a broader framework. But if we are to be capable of acting and thinking independently we must reach this ideology individually.

Pam

THE WOMEN'S MOVEMENT

A women's movement is necessary if this society is to be changed. As we recondition ourselves we must simultaneously resolve the contradictions in society. However, isolated groups cannot affect social change any more than can individuals. This is a political, social and psychological struggle and I do not believe that this is possible without a reorganization of society. We must question the viability of capitalism because we are exploited in the home as unpaid labor and in jobs as a cheap, reserve labor force, and we live in a society which exploits both people and nature for profit. We are also oppressed socially and psychologically and we must redefine men's and women's roles. For example, no liberation of women can take place without a redistribution of the responsibilities for home and child care. It is imperative that men and society assume some responsibility in both areas. In terms of housework this would mean both socializing many of the job functions and making them well paid jobs by professionals and sharing the other jobs equally among the family members. In terms of children it will mean society (and industry which should be socially owned rather than privately) would take over much of the early child care—creches, day care centers—and again, the individual family members sharing the rest equally.

Psychologically our liberation can only come by changing men's and women's male supremacist values and assumptions. This is very important. We have been socialized into a male supremacist culture and must resocialize ourselves, first by removing ourselves and organizing together and then reentering society with our demands and alternatives. To be independent in our thinking and to identify our interests as being those of all women, does not necessarily mean that we are anti-men. It simply means that we are free of their domination and know what are our own needs.

We do not allow men in our movement because in a male supremacist society men can and do act as the agents of our oppression. This takes not only obvious forms, such as physical and psychological brutality, but subtle forms as well, such as intellectual manipulation and maintaining concrete economic privileges. Even the most well intentioned man exists in a world which presumes his superiority; this clouds and colors his thinking to our detriment. It is not in our self interest to have men help us to define our needs; they cannot understand them. But this does not mean that we do not welcome their help. We do, but we wish to define that help. Child care is an example of where we think men's help is beneficial to all concerned. In addition we do recognize that this society exploits and dehumanizes many men. This, however, does not excuse their male supremacy, nor does it deter us from our first priority which is the needs and ideas of women. I would add, though, that I think the small group structure might prove very beneficial to men in helping them to find their humanity. I think it significant that very few men have seen fit to try a men's group experience. Men do not wish to assume the responsibility of being emotionally honest with themselves and each other; they have always used women as buffers and will continue to do so as long as we allow it. We do men no service by continuing to allow them to segregate their work and emotional lives, ignoring us in the former and using us in the latter. And we do ourselves no service draining our energies from our own fight by constantly meeting their needs. If we free men in the process of liberating ourselves (and we think we will) that is good, but our priority must be the liberation of women.

An autonomous women's movement will function to serve

women. This can happen in a number of ways. A women's movement needs to begin to develop a counter ideology and culture to male supremacy, which will affirm the basic human rights of all women and all people, including children. Secondly it must find ways of meeting the immediate needs of women so that they can grow and develop their fullest potentialities for the struggle. Third it must begin a systematic attack on male supremacist institutions which means every institution in the U.S. while simultaneously developing an interim program and long term goals. This last will necessitate preparing to take part in the leadership of the society along with other groups which are dedicated to the development of a society which meets the needs of all people, not a few, i.e. white males.

I think it important that people struggle for their own needs. We are, on the whole, middle class white women in our twenties and thirties. Our needs will be those of middle class women. A mass movement, if it is to represent the needs of all women, must reflect the needs of the most oppressed of our sisters. Therefore, the program of such a movement must be determined by poor women, and especially black and other non-white women for they are the most oppressed of our sisters. A mass movement will be made up of many organized groupings of women, each group expressing the needs of its constituency and coming together to struggle for goals beneficial to all women.

It will take us years to build such a women's movement. We are in the first steps. At present there are scattered organizations and groups of women all over the country but communication and cooperation are minimal. We need to increase honest communication with one another, and whenever possible we should come together to cooperate on common activities and programs, not refusing cooperation with any woman's group on specific issues unless there is disagreement on that issue. In our own area women in women's liberation have working relationships with the local chapters of the National Organization for Women and with Women Inc., a women's caucus in the Western Pulp and Paper Workers Union in Antioch and Stockton, California, as well as women's liberation groups in Berkeley, Palo Alto, and San Jose. No one women's group has the option on truth; there is no ideology which speaks to women's needs that has yet been evolved. Therefore we must consider ourselves in a formative period and that ideology will develop slowly through all of us working together towards the liberation of all women.

Ideology does not develop separate from action and programs. The definition of the small group as Free Space is based on this premise. The value of the small group is that it does offer a place to evaluate these experiments and to fit them into an overview. If the group is the place for women to develop their ideology, it would be most beneficial to the interaction within the group if the individual members were not all involved in the same political activities since the more experience that can be reported the better the chance for a comprehensive overview. In the same way that we value the perspective of our members that comes from their individual private lives, we in Sudsofloppen also value the perspective that comes from our members being involved in different projects within the women's movement in San Francisco.

In San Francisco the basic unit for women's liberation has been the small group. We help new women find groups through open orientation meetings. Our activities take the form of projects and direct actions which are cross-group—which have members who come from a number of small groups. We have conferences to communicate with one another and to discuss questions of interest. I anticipate that we will soon see the development of action organizations which will draw members from many small groups. I see this as a natural and healthy process, as one of the strengths of these organizations will be the small group membership of its participants for they will have a space to evaluate the progress of their organizations.

One of the reasons we feel that the small group structure is a good base for developing ideology is that groups can be at different stages depending on the needs of their members. Women new to the movement can participate in the early opening up and sharing processes together and not be prevented from having these important initial experiences by coming into a group which is already a functioning unit. At the same time women who have been in a group for a while will be free to grow further as they will not be forced to continually help new women reach their level of consciousness. This thinking does not assume that older groups will have the option on truth. Quite the contrary, leaving groups free to grow on their own gives them the option to deal with issues older groups may have been avoiding. In addition, individual women, whatever the age of their group, are free to join work projects as they feel ready. The group, because it is not a work project, will not put undue pressure on women to become active but will benefit greatly as each member begins to report back new experiences.

Not all small groups function according to the thinking of Sudsofloppen. Some have evolved different definitions of their function which, hopefully, they will begin to communicate to others. Other groups, however, have not been able to work out a satisfactory definition. We in San Francisco are not sure how to help women avoid stagnation and grow together by suggesting the use of the small group as Free Space. It is only one approach and may be workable in another group only after being adapted to the unique needs of that group.

The small group defined as Free Space offers a place to develop ideology but can only offer a place for perspective and support for women's other needs. A women's movement will need to find ways of fulfilling women's needs of a satisfactory private life and for meaningful work. In terms of private life needs this might be services towards helping women find satisfactory work (job referral), satisfactory living arrangements (housing service), sharing the responsibilities of child rearing (child care), meeting other women (social gatherings), and solving personal crises (counseling and therapy referral). But the basic responsibility must be the individual woman's. A women's movement cannot afford to divert the majority of its energies to helping individual women work out their private lives. The women's movement's first commitment is to changing the social conditions which make being female so oppressive. It is only by changing objective reality that all women will ever have the chance to be free.

In terms of meeting the need in individuals for creative work, the movement can do this in a number of ways. The process of building a mass movement of women and working towards changing our society, is socially productive work. Also, developing skills for the women's movement and offering services to other women is relevant work. Within a women's movement there should be numerous ways to contribute, but again the ultimate responsibility is on women themselves. The movement can suggest and even ask for workers in certain areas, but individual women must make the decision to give of their time and effort. Productive work is not easy and struggling towards our liberation will be frustrating and draining many times. The work will be time consuming and dreary but we will have our hope and our vision and there will be rewards along the way.

One last word about individual needs. A women's movement should encourage its members to grow in all areas simultaneously—the private life, work and idea areas. This means confronting the inequities in our personal lives as well as in society. How each woman chooses to make her stands and to make a more fulfilling life is her choice alone. The movement—and here Free Space is important—can help her work out what is correct for her as an individual both in terms of relationships with men and children and in terms of the type of work she will choose to engage in within the movement itself. But the decisions must be freely made by the individual woman herself, for she and not the movement must live her life. I have found that women do gain strength from the small group and will, when able, take new steps. If that growth is to be sustained, however, it must come from within the individual and not be a result of group pressure. This does not mean that the group should not confront a woman with the contradictions within herself but it does mean we must question whether the demands we make on others don't many times stem from our own needs and not theirs. If we believe in the liberation of all women and not just ourselves, we must be sensitive to the needs of others.

There are many ways to attack male supremacy. Women will probably choose to work on actions and projects that most fulfill their individual needs for creative work and for relieving the immediate oppression in their lives. It is clear that education, economic exploitation and abortion are already important fronts on which the battle is taking place. But regardless of what activities a woman chooses, it is imperative that she begin to evolve an overview within which to fit her actions. Thus again we return to the question of ideology and stress the importance of the small group as a place to effectively analyze and evaluate our political activities. The thread that runs through all our activity will be our ideology, or lack of one. We will succeed in building a mass movement of women, of changing the basic fabric of our society, if we have both a human and realistic understanding of ourselves and this society.

This means among other things that we must always take the personal needs of women into account when determining actions. These needs should not determine policy, but rather policies should incorporate personal needs. It is important to separate the personal needs from the decision making process in determining what tactics should be used in waging the battle for liberation. Individuals need to affirm their social worth and also to relieve their anger at their oppressors. But the ways chosen to meet these needs must be consistent with our commitment to alleviate the oppression of women. Our energies need to be channeled in ways which positively affect both the individual and the total movement whenever possible. For that we need an understanding of the numerous ways in which individual needs can be met, an understanding of the needs of our movement, and an understanding of the ways we can approach our goals successfully. For this we need an ideology.

Donna

THE STUDY PLAN

The importance of individuals developing an ideology has been stressed again and again in this handbook. It has been suggested that the small group, functioning as Free Space, is where this process can take place. One woman cannot know the total experience of women even with the help of written material. However, neither can one group. What follows is a study plan I have written which attempts to give structure to group meetings and encourages cross-group communication through monthly "collective" meetings. A central idea of this plan is that if a number of groups discuss the same subject matter all using the small group process, that communication and growth among individuals and between groups will be enhanced. We began this study plan in our group in February, 1970, and have found it very rewarding. I should note, however, that a new group which began the plan with us has found it necessary to adapt the plan slightly to meet their needs to get to know one another. We have found our "collective" meetings stimulating because of the variety and seriousness of the ideas brought here from the individual groups participating.

Juliet Mitchell in WOMEN: THE LONGEST REVOLUTION (reprinted from the Nov./Dec. 1966 *New Left Review* by the New England Free Press and the San Francisco Radical Education Project) identifies four elements of women's condition, all of which she feels are important for a comprehensive program aimed at making a society which meets the needs of women. These four elements are production, socialization, sexuality and reproduction.

We take each of these four elements and spend one month discussing the ways women are oppressed in each area, plus one month discussing how the four elements interrelate. Each time we use the small group process. This means we spend one week opening up about our feelings regarding that element, one week sharing our experiences, one week analyzing the situation using outside reading as well as our own experience and one week abstracting. On the fifth week we get together with the other groups doing the plan and share together our analysis and evolving theory. This will take at least six months, with one meeting each week.

After this we plan to spend an additional six months discussing the same four elements and how they relate in terms of our liberation. In other words, how will certain job functions be fulfilled, what type of society would be liberating for all its members, etc. Again we will use the small group process of opening up (our hopes and visions), sharing (our tentative explorations in living a more liberated life now), analyzing (how other societies are structured, what needs must be met) and abstracting (what would a liberated society look like). Again we will meet monthly with other groups using the same plan.

Then we will begin discussing how do we affect change; the interactions and weak points in the four elements in our society, and the necessary actions we must undertake. At this point we should have a very thorough and human understanding of women's condition and hopefully the beginning of a framework from which to act.

Two other things will be happening during this study program. We plan to leave time at each small group meeting for discussion of private life and job experiences. These should not be neglected. Information from both areas will help us in our study, for women's condition is not only an abstraction but a very real, subjective reality. Activity within our movement here in San Francisco will also give us leads as to effective and ineffective ways to organize projects. The small group experience is a meeting ground for all of our experiences as women; the study program is not divorced from this.

The oppression of women takes place on many levels. We are oppressed psychologically, socially and economically. The small group process will enable us to look at each element of women's condition in terms of all three levels of our oppression. The opening up experience is connected with our psychological oppression. Sharing combines the psychological with examples of social coercion. Analyzing combines the social coercion with economic exploitation and abstracting fits all three into a total framework, which includes the potentialities possible within a liberated life.

The class from which women come will partly determine the content of their thinking. Individual women have their female status in common but the ways they are oppressed in their home life (childhood and adult), their jobs and their psyches will depend both on their class and their individual opportunities to transcend that condition. Any study program that discusses the condition of women and has as its participants only middle class white females can only speak of the way those women are oppressed. The study program will be limited by the type of women who choose to participate. However, our first duty is to understand our own predicament, for then we will be clear about our motives for joining with other women in a mass movement. We will know now only that we are oppressed but how that oppression is accomplished.

An account of our current experience of the study plan would require more space than is available here. However, I would like to mention briefly one problem with which we are attempting to deal in our group and which is the subject of debate in much of the women's movement. This is the problem of defining the enemy. I think the answer to this problem will be multi-faceted; rather than defining one enemy we may find that we have many fronts and many levels on which to wage battle. Some of these are internal, within us, and regardless of their origin in society's values and institutions, they can cripple us and destroy us just as easily as can our enemies from without. I think at least five such enemies are easily identified and although I think all are prevalent in each of the four elements of women's condition, four do correspond roughly with the four elements. These are capitalism, men, ourselves and the state, and they correspond to production, sexuality, socialization and reproduction.

The fifth enemy, racism, is all pervasive and internally, probably our most dangerous enemy for it has historically separated women from each other allowing white women to seek privileges for themselves rather than making their cause with all women. A racist society such as ours imbues its racism in all its people. No one is exempt any more than any of us escapes the effects of male supremacy. The victims see the magnitude and subtleties of racism more clearly than those of us who benefit, whether by choice or not, from the privileges of being white. This is a truth we accept clearly regarding male supremacy and men. That is why we say that women must define their own needs and priorities themselves. We must be no kinder to ourselves regarding our racism that we are to men regarding their male supremacy. All overt examples of racism in our movement must be vigorously opposed and cannot be excused. The issue here is that programs for women's liberation must be beneficial to *all* women and have safeguards against their being used against any women. Our enemy is our arrogance, that we assume what benefits white women automatically benefits all women. We who have been privileged because of our color must learn to give up privileges we have at the expense of others at the same time as we fight for the rights which have been denied us as women.

THE FOUR ELEMENTS OF WOMEN'S CONDITION

PRODUCTION: Women do unpaid labor in the home for individual men but their basic exploitation is at the hands of capitalism for it is the low paying, menial job possibilities open to women which makes them dependent on men. It is profitable to pay women less money to work; it is possible because women are not organized. Businessmen will not give up their chance for profits without a fight. In addition men like having women in supportive roles, not in competitive ones. Thus there will be tremendous resistance to integrating women into any but support jobs. The issue here is the right of access to equal work. The enemy is the white male capitalists who control this society and benefit from the way it functions. Since profits are their aim, the needs of people, and especially women, come second. Already there is an unemployment problem. If all women demanded the right to equal work drastic changes would have to be made to meet their needs. This cannot happen as long as profits are the goal of production and not the needs of the people as a whole.

SEXUALITY: Since reproduction can now be separated from sex through birth control, sexuality is focussed on the relations between people of the same or opposite sex, and between individuals and their own bodies. The issue here is not only liberalization of the sexual mores for both men and women but also the basic questions of self image, equality and autonomy. So many examples of societies free of sexual inhibitions include the reduction of women to mere objects. This is true even of our own society, and true even of the alternative culture that hippies are trying to evolve. The enemy here is men, and women must fight to ensure that they maintain full autonomy in their relations with men. Only then will sexuality be liberating for women. Otherwise it is just an opiate for keeping the slaves happy.

SOCIALIZATION: The care of the very young has been

delegated to women. This is a very serious responsibility and ways found to relieve women and children of this inhuman bondage must take the very real needs of small children into account. Since women have done and continue to do the early socializing, we are our own worst enemies in this area. We have all the values and assumptions about the inherent inferiority of women socialized into us from birth by our mothers, most of whom preferred their male children to us. In addition unless we are careful, we will transfer these same attitudes towards self to our daughters. The issue here is our understanding of the complex mechanisms of socialization which begins with the very young and can be transmitted in non-verbal ways. Alternatives must be developed which deal with these subtleties.

REPRODUCTION: With birth control childbearing becomes one option among many for women. However, this is true only if birth control, including abortion and sterilization, is voluntary and is accessible to all women and men, and if other possibilities for self realization are open to women. The issue here is who controls women's bodies and determines what kind of children will be born. Up until now women have been prevented from terminating unwanted pregnancies except in a few privileged cases. But with concern rising over the population explosion, we will soon have to face the issue of population control. Meaningful work must be made available to women. Then, and only then, a voluntary goal of no increase in the population will be a possibility. We must protect the rights of poor and nonwhite women to bear children when they wish. The state cannot be allowed to determine which types of women should be allowed to have children. The enemy here is the state.

INTERRELATIONS: Entry of women into public industry on an equal basis is an absolute necessity, for all human beings need socially productive work and economic independence. Values are not changed by will alone but are very much related to the material base of a society. However, at the same time this must be accompanied by concrete changes in the elements of sexuality, socialization and reproduction if women are to be free. The basic unit of society—the nuclear family—will have to undergo drastic changes. Women will probably choose to work in actions which affect those elements that most oppress them as individuals. Thus young women will be concerned about reproduction, sexuality and production. Women with children will probably want more emphasis on socialization. Older women who have raised children will probably be most angry about the limited job opportunities open to them. Students and teachers will fight oppression in education—the channeling and miseducation of female students which prevents them from having either the skills or the self confidence to assume responsible jobs in production. But all women, regardless of the particular element that most oppresses them, need to have an overview of their total condition in this society as well as an understanding of how this society functions with its wars, devastation of natural resources and exploitation of peoples both here and abroad for the sake of profits for the few—the white males who run this country for their own ends, not for the needs of the people.

The study program is only a beginning to our understanding of our predicament. I think it is a productive beginning. It is important, however, that we remember that there are many obstacles to overcome before we can hope to achieve our goal of a free society. Women show signs of cooperation when working together on their own terms and not in male terms. I hope we will be able to emphasize these tendencies towards communalism and cooperation that women have shown throughout the ages and to minimize the exploitative tendencies which come when women isolate themselves as individuals against other women. If we maintain our commitment to the progress of all women and not only ourselves, if we can change our values from individualism to communalism, there is hope.

APPENDIX

One very important step in the process of uniting the political and personal concerns of our group by defining the function of our group as Free Space, was the experience of writing our ideas about what we hoped the group could be, first individually and then collectively. The collective paper, reprinted in edited form here, was written for a women's liberation conference in April 1969 and it was our first political action as a group. We took the name Sudsofloppen at this time. One of our members had used the name in her paper and we all felt that the concept of using a nonsense name was good because it would leave us plenty of room to grow and develop. No notion of who or what we were could be derived from the name separate from the work and ideas we produced.

The completion of the Sudsofloppen Paper gave us a tentative ideal toward which we wanted to struggle. This was frightening for all of us for we now knew what our commitment to one another meant. Not all were able to make that commitment and subsequently five of our members left us, four to go into other groups which more nearly suited their needs. We were now down to six members and we six, who represented both sides of the political versus personal debate, began together to try to put Free Space into practice.

THE SUDSOFLOPPEN PAPER

. . . This paper is being written because of our need to reach out. It resulted in strengthening our group by revealing the unity that even we were not quite sure was there. We shared a fear of expressing and writing our ideas but the work and commitment involved in producing the paper became a concrete example of what we are discovering about meaningful work. To structure something that comes from your guts is a very hard task.

We want to make it clear that the paper is a group effort. We each wrote a paper, met to make up the outline, met again to discuss the outline and split up sections to be written. When we met to compile the sections we were amazed at how easily they fit together without much editing. This gave testimony to our closeness . . .

Our group started out being very personal and as time went on and things began to bog down we found ourselves trying to look beyond our particular group to get some perspective. Trying to define the group was part of this—trying to see ourselves as a political form and not just Monday night meetings. We think this was a natural process.

Up to now we have been involved in a struggle between a personal emphasis that doesn't reach out versus a political emphasis lacking in substance. We've found a total emphasis on the personal a dead end. We don't want to lose the personal emphasis because it's an important way to measure the extent to which our ideas meet and come from needs. But again work, reaching out, is essential. We feel that the group used as a base for criticism and support is a way to combine these two needs.

We are a group of women who have realized that many of the assumptions which our society holds concerning women are not only limiting but damaging. We have all faced crises because in rejecting the society in which we have been reared, we are rejecting behavior which we have individually internalized. We cannot despise society's conception of women without despising many of the ways in which we and our friends behave. Therefore, we have been forces to try to identify and confront the societal demons within ourselves and to formulate conceptions which we see as more positive.

As women our important contacts with other people were confined to a one to one level. We needed this protection because we have been trained to be other directed, shaping our personalities to fit other people's expectations (projections). We could avoid rejection by closing off those facets of being not considered "feminine." We are now trying to forge a new form which would free us to be our real selves. We see that this free space—our group—is different from other groups in that it is not a place where you manipulate words divorced from reality to manufacture a public image such as in the classroom or political meeting; this is not a place which ties you down to acting in set patterns; this is not a place involved simply in analysis of those set patterns, sharpening our understanding but leaving us bound.

Our group is laboring towards building a collective trust. The realization of this trust will come with the understanding that we are committed to opening those potentialities we had closed off. We are involved in a tentative, groping exploration that we could open ourselves to passionate creativity. The move from alienation to commitment involves a terrifying lowering of defenses; all of us have considered pulling out. The bleakness of our lives coupled with a collective hope that this would be a meaningful alternative has sufficed to keep the group together. The life of the individual and the group are no longer segregated (alienated); as the individuals find new confidence and sense of self worth, so the group is affirming itself by becoming engaged in serious meaningful action.

Many of us were becoming more and more demoralized as we saw ourselves unable to fit our new concepts of ourselves as women into our daily lives. The more aggressive would rush head on into confrontations or discussions with other only to be hurled back in utter defeat; while the more passive knew they could never live up to their new ideals and didn't even try. So we would come back to meetings hating ourselves for having failed each other and our ideals. Slowly we are coming to accept the necessity for moving one step at a time, working first on those aspects of ourselves which are most easy to change and accepting the need for compromise in other areas for the time being.

We now see the group as a place where we can isolate specific areas of compromise, look at the situations objectively and analyze the most productive form of attack. For those of us who rush headlong into things, we can come back with reports of how we fared and receive sympathetic advice on how we could have better handled the situation or even why we should have left well enough alone. And for those of us who withdraw from such situations, the group can help us to see in what ways we are capable of standing our ground.

So the group is a free space where we can withdraw from the daily struggles for a while and gain perspective on ourselves and the roles we play in our private and public lives.

This group has had a radicalizing effect on us. Now we understand in our gut something we used to give only lip service to: that there is no personal solution to being a woman in this society. We have realized that if we do not work to change the society it will in the end destroy us. We are able to look back at our adolescence and see that we each felt that we could escape the traps that the women around us had fallen into. But now we are aware that those escape routes narrow with age; there are fewer and fewer ways to keep from falling into the normal patterns of behavior. And so the group becomes an essential unit in our fight to create alternatives.

. . . We began to look at ourselves and the people immediately around us to see how they had contributed to our dehumanization. Although we recognized the roles that ourselves, parents, teachers and friends play in this process, we turned our attention specifically on the men in our lives. We recognized that these were the people who had the most influence on our ways of thinking. Then we went through a rather long period of venting our resentments and hostilities on the men who oppressed us in our daily lives. As we now look back on that period we see it as a healthy process through which we had to pass in order to free ourselves from our own bitterness and to gain an understanding of the interpersonal dynamics between men and women which work to the detriment of women. It is not within the scope of this paper to discuss the ways in which the male-female relationship works against us. We are not saying that these are necessarily conscious dynamics. Rather, men and women many times act according to socially prescribed roles which have been unconsciously internalized and, in a male supremacist society like ours, this is always to the detriment of women.

We are no longer as concerned with male chauvinism as we are much more concerned with our relationships with other women. As we have become strengthened in our concepts of ourselves we have, to a great extent, freed ourselves from the inordinate amount of influence men have over the thinking of women. We are much freer now to look to other women for support but also to recognize which female roles oppress ourselves and other women. We are beginning to see how we act as agents of our own oppression through seeing other women as rivals rather than sisters

61

and have become very committed to developing a sisterhood among ourselves as a group and with other groups of women. We see any political activity we might choose to engage in to advance our cause as women as growing out of this sisterhood.

We are aware that our own self-hatred is one of our chief enemies. Our group has had to come to the realization that there are certain aspects of self-hatred, such as the drive toward suicide, that brings the group to a point of impasse. We have discovered that talking about certain problems such as suicide is not as helpful as isolating specific oppressed ways of thinking and behaving with which we are able to deal. For instance, the specific oppressed ways of behaving that we have approached by writing this paper are our weaknesses in conceptualization, writing, theorizing and taking ourselves seriously. Our group then is hopefully becoming a place where women whose lives are so meaningless can begin to find meaningful activity.

With this new move, we're discovering a number of varied interests and talents within our group. At first this leads to a fear of disunity. But women discovering their unfulfilled potential is a reason for joy and not fear. Unity must come from working together and not like-mindedness. Working together strengthens the group to become a place that provides direction for the individual to discover both the ability to meet her own individual needs and her role in meeting needs in the women's movement.

The group can become a place for us to get encouragement, help, and support to learn, grow and act, and a place to come back to for criticism for we want to learn from our mistakes. Since our group has felt the need to reach out—through conferences and contact with other groups and individuals—we are seeing that a movement is beginning to develop. We see the need now for more contact with groups locally and this direction is going to lead to the need for contact with groups nationally. As the movement gets larger it is essential that every woman answer to her group and always be a representative of that group so that she can neither be singled out for glory nor suppression . . .

Sudsofloppen
San Francisco
April 19, 1969

OTHER TITLES FROM TIMES CHANGE PRESS

This Woman: Poetry of Love & Change, Barbara O'Mary/$1.50
Lessons from the Damned: Class Struggle in the Black Community/$2.75
Amazon Expedition: A Lesbian/Feminist Anthology/$1.75
Begin At Start: Personal Liberation & World Change, Su Negrin/$2.75
Youth Liberation: News, Politics & Survival Information/$1.75
Free Space: The Small Group in Women's Liberation, Pamela Allen/$1.35
Great Gay in the Morning!: On Communal Living & Sexual Politics/$2.25
The Tupamaros: Urban Guerrillas of Uruguay, Carlos Núñez/$1.00
Generations of Denial: 75 Biographies of Women, Kathryn Taylor/$1.35
Unbecoming Men: A Men's Group Writes on Oppression & Themselves /$1.75
Some Pictures from My Life: A Woman's Diary, Marcia Salo Rizzi/$1.35
Ecology & Revolutionary Thought, Murray Bookchin/$1.25
Woodhull & Claflin's Weekly: On Feminism, Socialism & Mysticism/$1.35
Come Out!: Selections from the Radical Gay Liberation Newspaper/$1.25
Free Ourselves: Forgotten Goals of the Revolution, Arthur Aron/$1.35
The Traffic in Women and Other Essays on Feminism, Emma Goldman/$1.35
Honor America: The Nature of Fascism, Stanley Aronowitz/75¢
Listen to the Mocking Bird: Satiric Songbook, Tuli Kupferberg / $1.50
Burn This & Memorize Yourself: Poems for Women, Alta/50¢
The Cultural Revolution: A Marxist Analysis, Irwin Silber/$1.25
Somos/We Are: Five Contemporary Cuban Poets/$1.00
A Graphic Notebook on Feminism, Su Negrin/$1.25
Arab-Israeli Debate: Toward a Socialist Solution/$1.25
The Fat Capitalist's Song on the Death of Che Guevara, Anon. poem/50¢
Hip Culture: Six Essays on Its Revolutionary Potential/$1.25

To order any of the above, send cash, check or money order (made out to Times Change Press), plus 35¢ for postage and handling, to **Times Change Press, c/o Monthly Review Press, 62 W. 14th St., NYC 10011.**

POSTERS ARE ALSO AVAILABLE

On Feminism, Third World Struggles, Gay Liberation, etc. They are $1 each and are all illustrated in our free catalog.

WRITE FOR OUR FREE ILLUSTRATED CATALOG
Times Change Press—Catalog Dept.
c/o Monthly Review Press, 62 W. 14th St., NYC 10011